Pet Expert

HORSES & PONIES

By Gemma Barder

PET EXPERT:
HORSES AND PONIES!

If you love horses and ponies they you have certainly picked up the right book. The following pages are packed with essential horse and pony information from how to look after your pony to how humans and ponies first started to live together. Horses and ponies are amazing creatures, but did you know just how amazing? Throughout this book you'll learn about famous horses, record-breaking horses as well as some truly fascinating horsey facts. In fact, let's start right now!

CONTENTS

RARE
BREEDS

PONY
PROTOCOL

HORSE-
KEEPING!

ANIMAL
BABIES

HUNDREDS OF HORSES

Horses and ponies come in different shapes and sizes, each with their own unique personalities. Find out all about the differences between our equine friends here.

WHICH IS IT?

It can be tricky to tell the difference between a horse and a pony. Usually, ponies are shorter than horses. Any adult equine that is shorter than 14.2 hands is most-likely to be a pony – but there are exceptions to the rule (find out about miniature horses later in the book!).

DID YOU KNOW?

The unit used to measure horses and ponies is called a hand, which is about 10.16 cm. You measure their height from the top of their withers (shoulder blades) to the ground.

HORSES vs PONIES

There are lots of factors that make ponies and horses different:

- For their size, ponies are stronger than horses.
- Horses are faster than ponies.
- Ponies are generally believed to be cleverer than horses.
- Horses grow more slowly than ponies.
- Ponies tend to have thicker manes and coats than horses.
- Horses need a lot more food than ponies.
- Ponies live longer than horses.

Horses and ponies are both part of the equine family, but they are different animals.

HORSES AND PONIES

See if you can spot the difference between a pony and a horse the next time you pass a paddock or go to the stables.

SHIRE HORSES

These are gentle giants. Their average height is 17 hands (173 cm), but they can grow much larger. You can spot a shire by its trademark shaggy hooves and muscular frame – perfect for heavy work, such as pulling tree trunks, ploughs or brewery carts! These calm horses don't get spooked easily.

DID YOU KNOW?

Shire horses got their name because they were first bred in the UK in LincolnSHIRE and CambridgeSHIRE.

THOROUGHBRED

A thoroughbred has long legs, a sleek coat and a lean body – perfect for horse racing and other high-speed sports, such as polo. They are called 'hot blooded' because of their strong and spirited nature and can grow to around 16 hands (163 cm). They are also expensive – young racehorses are sold for millions.

SHETLAND PONY

Shetland ponies grow to around eight hands (81 cm) and they can pull up to twice their own weight! Their small, powerful frames meant they were sent to work in cramped coal mines in Britain and the USA. Today, Shetland ponies are the ideal riding ponies for small children.

DID YOU KNOW?

All thoroughbreds are recorded as having one of two birthdays (1st January or 1st August) even if they aren't born on these dates!

DID YOU KNOW?

Some Shetland ponies have been trained as guides for the blind.

HARD-TO-FIND HORSES

There are hundreds of different breeds of horses and ponies in the world, with many on the endangered list. Read on to discover some you might not have heard of!

Caspian horses are great at jumping and are a top choice for young showjumpers!

AMERICAN CREAM

This is a draft horse, which means it is big and strong like a shire. The colour of its coat is called 'champagne gold', which is a mixture of the more common colours, champagne and chestnut. American creams have amazing eyes, which are almost white at birth, then turn amber.

CASPIAN

One of the most ancient breeds of horses still around today, Caspians were thought to be extinct until they were re-discovered in Iran in 1965. Although Caspians are small compared to other horses (around 11 hands) they are still classed as horses because of the way they look.

There are just 250 American creams left in the world today.

HACKNEY

Owning a hackney horse and carriage 200 years ago was like owning a Ferrari today. The reason they were so popular was their unique high trot and majestic features. When carriages began to be swapped for motor cars, the hackney lost its popularity and in 2012 it was added to the critical list for endangered breeds.

FACT FILE

STUNNING: AKHAL TEKE
These golden-coloured horses are the national symbol of Turkmenistan, where they originate from. They form a really strong bond with whoever rides them first and don't like to change owners.

GRACEFUL: LIPIZZAN
For centuries, this beautiful grey horse has been bred for dressage - a kind of riding where the horse and rider perform a series of special movements. Although adult Lipizzans are grey, they are born black or brown.

60 million

350 breeds

There are approximately 60 million horses on the planet, and there are over 350 different breeds of horse.

DID YOU KNOW?
In the horse world, white-coloured horses are always called greys.

BODY LANGUAGE

Horses and ponies give us lots of clues to how they are feeling. All you have to do is look carefully and read the signs.

THE BIG PICTURE

Take a step back and look at your horse to see how they are feeling. If their muscles are tensed and they have stiff movements, it could be that they are in pain, nervous or stressed.

TAIL

A raised tail can indicate that your horse or pony is excited and ready for fun. If the tail is clamped down against its bottom, it usually means the horse is upset or anxious about something around them. Swishing shows irritation.

Horses can sleep standing up, so be careful when greeting a horse with its eyes closed - they could be having a quick snooze!

HINDLEGS

Stepping behind the powerful back legs of a pony can be dangerous, so make sure you keep clear at all times - even if you think your pony is calm. If one leg is lifted, your pony is showing you that they are upset or spooked.

EARS ▫

If the ears are pricked up it means the horse is alert and happy. However, if the ears are turned out to the side it could be that the horse is sleepy or 'zoned-out'. If the ears are flicking forwards and backwards or are pinned back towards the neck, your horse may not be very happy.

DID YOU KNOW?

Horses and ponies can see around 350 degrees because of the position of their eyes on either side of their head. This means they can see most of what is around them at all times.

▫ EYES

Most of the time, only the pupil and the iris of the eye can be seen. However, if you start to see the white part of a horse's eyes, it can be a sign that they are scared or upset.

▫ HEAD

A horse or pony who holds its head up is alert and aware of everything around it. If the head is lowered, it's a good sign your horse or pony is chilling out – or they could even be asleep! A horse that swishes its head and neck from side to side like a snake could be feeling aggressive, so be very careful around them.

FORELEGS ▫

When a horse or pony is digging with one of its front hooves (pawing) it usually indicates that they want something. They may also stamp their front legs from time to time to show frustration and anger.

FOALS

We all know baby horses and ponies are super-cute, but did you know they also develop really quickly and learn lots in just their first year? Read on to discover more!

FIRST STEPS

Foals can stand up and take their first steps just two hours after they are born. It can take human babies around a year to do this!

Have you ever noticed how long a foal's legs are? That's because they are almost the same length they will be when they are fully grown.

GROWING STRONG

Milk gives a young foal everything it needs for the first three months of its life, but it can also start eating grass at six weeks.

Foals and their mothers bond very quickly and stay together for at least six months until the foal is weaned.

FACT FILE

■ All baby horses and ponies are called foals.

■ A female foal is called a filly.

■ A male foal is called a colt.

■ After about a year, foals are called yearlings.

■ Yearlings become adult horses or ponies when they are three or four years old.

DID YOU KNOW?

Foals can be born with 16 teeth! (Adult horses have up to 40 teeth.)

10%   90%

A healthy foal should weigh the same as 10% of its mother's weight. Within 24 months they will grow to around 90% of their adult size.

SPRING INTO LIFE

It takes 11 months for a foal to grow inside its mother before it is ready to come into the world. Horse breeders like foals to be born in the springtime so they can spend the spring and summer months running around outside getting big and strong.

HORSE-KEEPING

Looking after a horse or pony is lots of fun, but there's also plenty of hard work to be done! To help you prepare, here's a start-up guide to looking after your equine friend.

HOOF CARE

Hooves should be inspected and cleaned out frequently, especially after a long ride or hack. If your horse or pony gets something lodged in their hoof, or if their shoe slips, it can be very uncomfortable and lead to problems in their legs and back.

FOOD AND DRINK

Horse and ponies eat a mixture of forage, and food such as oats, grains and pellets. They should be allowed to graze on forage as much as they want. Fresh water is also really important, so make sure their trough is always clean and topped up.

HEALTH CHECK

It's very important to check your horse or pony each day and let a vet know if you think they are unwell. Like many animals, horses and ponies need to be wormed regularly and given vaccinations against diseases and viruses, such as horse flu.

DID YOU KNOW?

'Forage' is another word for grass and hay.

DID YOU KNOW?

Horses and ponies need to be taken to a special person, called a farrier, every six weeks to have their hooves trimmed and their shoes replaced.

MANE ATTRACTION

If your horse's mane is loose (not tied up), you will need to make sure it is kept clean and free from tangles. Use a special horse brush to make sure the mane stays neat. You can also learn how to braid and knot your pony's mane to keep it tidy and free from mud.

Make sure you clean your horse's brushes frequently and don't use them on other horses. Sharing brushes can spread infections.

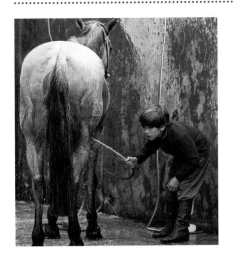

KEEPING CLEAN

The best way to keep your pony clean is to brush them every day and give them a good wash whenever they need it. Brushing your horse gets rid of dirt as well as helping you to develop trust and friendship with your favourite animal.

TEETH AND GUMS

Although it's hard to see all of a horse's teeth, you can still keep an eye on how they are developing. Watch out for changes in the teeth and any irritation. You should also keep track of how your pony's breath smells! If it gets super-smelly it could be a sign of disease.

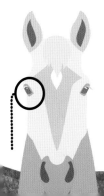

DID YOU KNOW?

Once a year, horses and ponies should be seen by an equine dentist.

PONY PROTOCOL

There are lots of things to remember when looking after a horse or pony. Take a look at these top dos and don'ts.

DO:

give your horse or pony plenty of exercise. ✔

make sure they have plenty of outside space to roam in and a warm, dry stable. ✔

groom your horse's coat, mane and tail every day. ✔

look at your horse's face for clues to how it is feeling – it is super expressive! ✔

keep your pony's trough clean and topped up – they needs lots of water! ✔

make sure they have plenty of grass and hay to graze on. ✔

stroke their nose to say hello. ✔

keep your horse with others – they get lonely if they don't have companions. ✔

DON'T:

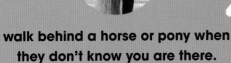

walk behind a horse or pony when they don't know you are there.

feed them mouldy or dusty hay.

ride them with poorly fitting tack.

let anyone too big ride a small horse or pony.

forget to check their hooves and teeth daily.

leave toxic plants, such as ragwort, in their paddock.

FOOD FOR HORSES

 grass

 carrots

 chocolate

 potatoes

 hay

 bananas

 garlic

 tomatoes

 apples

 celery

 onions

 meat

THE PERFECT STABLE

Most of your horse or pony's time should be spent in a large paddock with at least one friend. When they come inside, here are some top tips on giving them the cosiest stable to spend the night in.

BEDDING

Give your horse somewhere cosy to snuggle up in at night. Horse bedding is traditionally made out of straw, but you can also use special shredded paper, wood chippings or wood pellets.

FOOD AND DRINK

Horses and ponies need a constant supply of water and food to graze on. Your stable should have a raised haynet or trough for food and a good supply of water to keep your horse happy until it's time to go outside again.

SPACE

A stable box, or stall, should be big enough for your horse to move around in comfortably. The British Horse Society advises that boxes or stalls should be at least 3.6 m x 3.6 m for a horse and at least 3 m x 3 m for a pony.

MUCKING OUT

Mucking out is the name given to clearing out your pony's stable. How often you muck out will depend on how long your pony spends in their stable. You will need to clear out any poo and wet bedding each day and replace it with clean, dry bedding for your horse to sleep on.

HELLO THERE!

All stables have a stable door (or Dutch door) that can be closed at the bottom, while the top half stays open. These doors make sure that lots of fresh air gets into the stable, while letting your curious horse have a look outside whenever it wants to.

TROT THROUGH TIME

Horses and ponies have been helping humans for thousands of years. From pulling chariots to fighting in wars, find out how horses and ponies have helped shape the world.

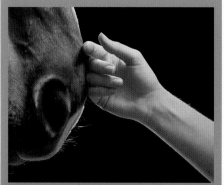

PICTURE THAT!

The first drawings showing humans riding horses are 4,000 years old and come from the Middle East. As well as being ridden, the images show that horses were also used for milk and meat.

4500 BCE | **2000 BCE** | **CE 100**

LONG-TERM RELATIONSHIP

The first evidence of horses being domesticated (tamed to live alongside humans) is over 6,000 years ago. Archaeological evidence from Ukraine (Eastern Europe) and Kazakhstan (Central Asia) shows large numbers of horses living with humans.

SUPER-FAST HIGHWAY

Once humans figured out they could ride horses, they were able to travel a lot faster and carry more things with them. As soon as horses were hitched to carts, huge amounts of people began buying and selling products, and soon the first roads were invented for horses and carts to ride along.

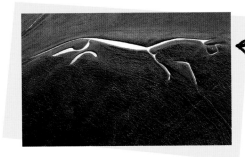

The White Horse is constantly cleaned by a team of volunteers. If it wasn't, it would disappear in just a few days!

TRANSPORT TO SPORT

In 1698, the steam engine was invented and just over 100 years later the first steam trains appeared. Horses began to be used less and less for transport and more and more for sport and leisure. Once cars and lorries hit the roads, horses were no longer used for taking goods around the country.

NYPD

1200s

1800s

2000s

BRED FOR SUCCESS

Horses and ponies were used for lots of different tasks. Some needed to be strong to work in the fields, or fast to deliver messages, and others needed to be brave and tough for the battlefield. This is how many of our modern-day breeds came into being.

HORSES TODAY

Horses and ponies are still an important part of life. They are used by the police and the army, and in lots of different sports, such as racing and show jumping. But most importantly, they are still beloved family pets!

FAMOUS FRIENDS

Horses are incredible animals. It's no wonder they are the stars of legendary tales, best-selling novels and sports worldwide.

BUCEPHALUS

Bucephalus is the legendary horse of Alexander the Great (356–323 BCE), the mighty king who united Greece and conquered the Persian Empire. Everyone thought Bucephalus was untameable, so Alexander asked his owner if he could keep the horse if he was able to ride him. Bucephalus is said to be the bravest horse in history.

ECLIPSE

Eclipse, who lived from 1764 until 1789, is one of the most famous racehorses in history. During his racing career he was undefeated, and eventually had to stop racing as no one wanted to run against him! All today's thoroughbreds can trace their bloodline back to this awesome horse.

DID YOU KNOW?

Eclipse had a larger-than-average heart, which he passed down to some of his descendants, including another legendary racehorse from the 1970s called Secretariat.

BLACK BEAUTY

Black Beauty is probably the world's most famous book about a horse. It was written in 1877 by Anna Sewell and tells the tale of a beautiful jet-black horse throughout his life. It is famous for being one of the first ever books to talk about animal welfare and it is recommended by the RSPCA.

WAR HORSE

War Horse tells the story of Joey, a farm horse who is sold to the army, leaving his owner and best friend, Albert behind. It was written in 1982 by Michael Morpurgo and since then it has been adapted into an award-winning stage play and a film directed by Steven Spielberg.

PRIZE-WINNING PONIES

These incredible horses have made their name in the *Guinness Book of Records*. Discover more about these unique animals!

CLEVEREST HORSE

One very clever thoroughbred called Lukas got into the *Guinness Book of Records* for identifying 19 numbers in 60 seconds! He didn't have a very good start in life and his trainer believes this amazing horse is proof that with love and attention we can all thrive.

HIGHEST-JUMPING HORSE

The highest jump by a horse ever recorded was back in 1949, in Chile. The horse was called Huaso Ex-Faithful and it jumped to a huge height of 2.47 m.

$70 million

$8,000

$70 million was the price paid for Fusaichi Pegasus, the world's most expensive racehorse, in 2000.

$8,000 was the price paid for legendary, champion racehorse Seabiscuit in 1936.

SEABISCUIT

FASTEST HORSE

A racehorse called Winning Brew was clocked going 70.76 kph at the Penn National Race Course in Pennsylvania, USA, in 2008.

TALLEST HORSE

Big Jake is the world's tallest horse at just over 20 hands, or 203 cm, which is taller than most professional basketball players! He makes use of his large size by helping out on a farm in Michigan, USA. According to his owner, Big Jake is a friendly horse and is loved by all the other farm animals!

Big Jake

Thumbelina

SMALLEST HORSE

The world's smallest horse is a Miniature Sorrel called Thumbelina. She stands at a teeny 44.5 cm, which means she is just over four hands tall!

THE PONY LOWDOWN

Ever wondered why your pony never needs to lie down, or what to give it for a special treat? Get ready to discover five things you never knew about horses!

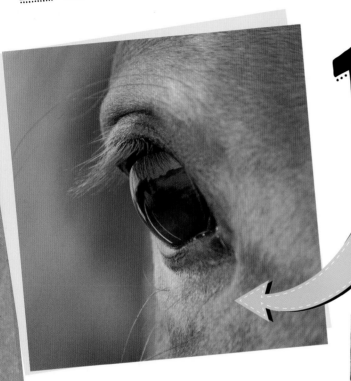

1 THEY HAVE REALLY BIG EYES!

Horses and ponies have the largest eyes of any mammal on land. Their pupils are horizontal slits and their eyes can see nearly 350 degrees. Their eyes developed this way to make sure they could see any predators coming for them when they were grazing in the wild!

2 THEY HAVE UNIQUE KNEES!

Horses and ponies can sleep standing up because of a special locking mechanism in their knees that stops them from falling over.

3 THEIR NAME MEANS 'ODD-TOED HORSE'

The scientific name for a horse is *equus ferus caballus* meaning 'odd toed horse' because horses technically have one toe on each foot (their hoof).

4 THEIR EARS ARE LIKE THERMOMETERS

You can take a horse's temperature by placing your hand behind their ear. Some parts of a horse's body will naturally feel cooler than others, but the temperature behind their ears will give you a good idea of their overall body temperature.

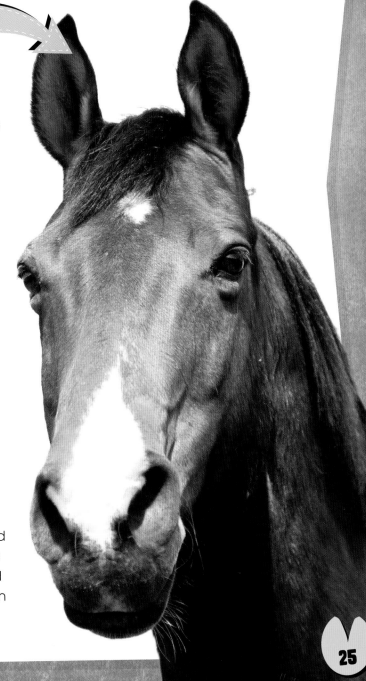

5 THEY HAVE A SWEET TOOTH

They love sweet-tasting things. Horses and ponies like treats, such as mints, bananas and even sugar cubes – but these should be given as occasional treats as they can be bad for their teeth.

YOUR PERFECT PONY

Which of these horses and ponies best reflects the type of person you are? Follow the flow to find out!

DO YOU LOVE TO READ?

Yes →

ARE YOU CALM IN A CRISIS?

Sometimes

Usually

Not always!

Sometimes

ARE YOU QUIET IN CLASS?

Yes

ARE YOU ON A SPORTS TEAM?

No

Yes

DO YOU ALWAYS LOOK YOUR BEST?

Mostly

Of course

DO YOU STICK UP FOR YOURSELF?

Definitely

Sometimes

DO ALL GOOD THINGS COME IN SMALL PACKAGES?

Yes

No

Sometimes

No

DO YOU LOVE TO TAKE CHARGE?

Slow

ARE YOU SLOW AND STEADY OR FAST AND FURIOUS?

Fast

SHETLAND

These little ponies may seem sweet, but they are strong and determined. Just like you, they won't let anyone down, and they love being around people.

SHIRE HORSE

Shire horses are the big, friendly, giants of the equine world. They quietly help others and like to observe the world around them.

THOROUGHBRED

These swift, sleek horses need lots of care, attention and exercise, which is perfect because so do you. You're the perfect match for these energetic equines!

QUIZ!

Now you've learned all about horses and ponies, are you a true equine expert? Answer the questions to find out.

1 HANDS ARE USED TO MEASURE HORSES AND PONIES. HOW BIG IS A HAND?

a) 5 cm
b) 10.16 cm
c) 15 cm

2 HOW MANY AMERICAN CREAM HORSES ARE LEFT IN THE WORLD?

a) 250
b) 2,500
c) 25,000

3 WHAT DO HORSES AND PONIES DO WITH THEIR EARS WHEN THEY ARE ANXIOUS?

a) prick them up
b) let them hang to the side
c) flick them backwards and forwards

4 HOW LONG DOES IT TAKE FOR A FOAL TO STAND UP AFTER BEING BORN?

a) 2 hours
b) 2 days
c) 2 weeks

5 WHY SHOULDN'T YOU USE YOUR HORSE'S GROOMING BRUSH ON OTHER HORSES?

a) horses get jealous if their brushes are used on others
b) you could spread infection
c) it makes the bristles weak

The answers can be found on page 30.

6 WHAT IS THE BEST WAY TO SAY HELLO TO YOUR HORSE?

a) a shout and a big wave
b) walk in backwards
c) gently stroke their nose

9 WHO WROTE *BLACK BEAUTY*

a) Anna Sewell
b) Enid Blyton
c) J.K. Rowling

7 WHAT IS ANOTHER NAME FOR A STABLE DOOR?

a) a French door
b) a Dutch door
c) a German door

10 WHAT'S THE NAME OF THE WORLD'S SMALLEST HORSE?

a) Thumbelina
b) Pixie
c) Titch

8 APPROXIMATELY HOW MANY HORSES ARE ON THE PLANET?

a) 20 million
b) 40 million
c) 60 million

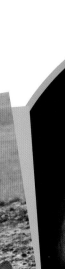

GLOSSARY

COLT
A young, male horse.

DRESSAGE
An artistic form of horse riding, performed at competitions.

ENDANGERED
A species of animal that is at risk of extinction.

EQUINE
From the Latin word for horse. Anything relating to horses or ponies.

FARRIER
Someone who specialises in horses' shoes who fits them to the horse.

FILLY
A young, female horse.

FOAL
A horse that is typically under a year old.

FORAGE
Grass or hay eaten by a horse to keep its tummy working properly.

GRAZE
Eating lightly throughout the day.

HANDS
A unit of measurement used to measure horses.

HOOF
A horse's foot.

HORSE POWER
Used to measure the power of an engine compared to the power of a horse.

MANE
The hair that grows along the neck of a horse.

MUCKING OUT
Clearing out any soiled hay and cleaning up a stable.

NORSE
Norwegians or Scandinavians in ancient or medieval times.

PADDOCK
A small field for horses to exercise.

RAGWORT
A wildflower poisonous to horses and ponies.

STABLE
The building where horses are housed.

TACK
Equipment used to ride a horse, including saddle, stirrups and bridle.

TRAINER
Someone who trains a horse to run fast or perfect a skill (such as dressage).

TROUGH
A long, deep container for horses and ponies to drink out of.

WEANED
When a horse can live off food alone, instead of its mother's milk.

YEARLING
A horse that is between one and two years old.

QUIZ ANSWERS

1. B,   2. A,   3. C,   4. A,   5. B,   6. C,   7. B,   8. C,   9. A,   10. A.

INDEX

Published in paperback in Great Britain in 2020 by Wayland

Copyright © Hodder and Stoughton, 2019

Editor: Dynamo Limited

Designer: Dynamo Limited

ISBN: 978 1 5263 0819 1

Printed and bound in China

Wayland, an imprint of

Hachette Children's Group

Part of Hodder and Stoughton

Carmelite House

50 Victoria Embankment

London EC4Y 0DZ

An Hachette UK Company

www.hachette.co.uk

www.hachettechildrens.co.uk

FSC
www.fsc.org

MIX
Paper from
responsible sources
FSC® C104740

Picture acknowledgements:

All images courtesy of Getty Images iStock apart from: P3 tr P6 cr Bob Langrish/Alamy, P6 bl P29 br Joel Sartore/National Geographic/Alamy, P7 t Juniors Bildarchiv GmbH/Alamy, P19 tr Charles Walker Collection/ Alamy, P20 bl Joel Sartore/National Geographic/Alamy, P21 br Geraint Lewis/Alamy, P23 tr M & N/Alamy
(Key: tr-top right, t-top, cr-centre right, bl-bottom left, br-bottom right)